SCHOLAST

M000107077

Revision Grade 6
Mini-Lessons

By Sarah Glasscock

NEW YORK • TORONTO • LONDON • AUCKLAND • SYDNEY **Teaching**
MEXICO CITY • NEW DELHI • HONG KONG • BUENOS AIRES *Resources*

Cover Design by Jaime Lucero

Interior Design by Sydney Wright

Interior Illustrations by Kelly Kennedy

ISBN-13 978-0-439-70490-8
ISBN-10 0-439-70490-1
Copyright © 2006 by Sarah Glasscock
All rights reserved.
Printed in the U.S.A.

1 2 3 4 5 6 7 8 9 10   40   14 13 12 11 10 09 08 07 06

CONTENTS

INTRODUCTION

One of the most difficult things about writing is making sure that we have successfully translated the ideas in our head to the words on the page. The goal in writing is to communicate effectively so that the reader is transported and not disappointed or confused. Revising is an essential part of the writing process. By going over what we've written, we show ownership of and pride in our words.

How to Use This Book

This book revolves around 13 topics that students often experience difficulties with in their writing. While some students become adept at catching errors as they work, others write without ever looking back at what they've written. Yet every writer benefits from taking the time to revise a piece of writing.

Each lesson contains a passage with errors for students to revise. A variety of genres and curriculum links are represented in the passages. To serve as a reference for students, a cartoon and a reminder about a key aspect of the topic appear above each passage. The first error in each passage is corrected on the page. When you begin teaching these lessons, I suggest that you read aloud the passage as students follow along. By using the rhythm of your voice and intonation, you'll be able to highlight the errors in a passage, for example, making your delivery flat as you read a series of repeated nouns or stumbling over misspelled words.

The corresponding teaching page contains a bulleted list of common errors associated with the topic, a review section called Replay, troubleshooting tips, and a section with suggestions about how to present the passage and model the correction shown. These are only suggestions—feel free to tailor the lesson to the needs of your students and your own teaching style.

After you and your students have discussed the passage, it's their turn to become editors. There is space for students to mark their changes directly on the passage reproducible. A checklist appears at the bottom of this page as a guide for students. Before students copy their revision on the blank reproducible page, have them write it out on a separate sheet of paper. This will give them some leeway to revise more before they actually publish their final draft.

Sample revisions appear in an answer key at the back of the book, along with a writing checklist found on page 48. A list of proofreader's marks is on page 5. Make sure students are familiar with and comfortable using the proofreader's marks before they tackle the passages.

Encourage your students to make these passages their own. Although the focus of a passage may be on subject-verb agreement, they should make any other changes they feel would strengthen the passage.

I hope this book helps your students—and you—feel that revision can be a pleasure.

Proofreader's Marks

Symbol	Meaning	Example
∧	Add a word or phrase	The ∧ puppy sighed. *lonely* The puppy sighed∧. *in his sleep*
ꬶ	Delete a letter or a word	The dark chocolate brown puppy yappℯ̶d. The ~~deep, dark~~ chocolate brown puppy yapped.
≡	Capitalize	The active puppies at pet world tumbled in their pen.
/	Lowercase	My D̸ad brought home a Border Collie puppy.
∪	Transpose letters	Border collies are one of the smartest breesd of dogs.
⊙ ⑦ ⑴	Change end punctuation	Do you have any pets∧ ⑦ I have two dogs and three hamsters⑨
¶	Begin a new paragraph	¶My dog, Buster, loves to jump on the couch. He enjoys watching TV with me.

Teamwork: SUBJECT-VERB AGREEMENT

Passage "All in a Day's Work" (realistic fiction)

Curriculum Area Language Arts

Subjects and verbs are the heart and soul of sentences. They work together as a singular team or a plural team. When students revise their work, they must make sure that the subjects and verbs still agree and remain on the same team.

Your students may encounter the following problems with subjects and verbs in their writing:

- Omitting a subject and a verb in a sentence.
- Choosing the wrong form of a verb to go with a subject.
- Difficulty identifying compound subjects and compound verbs.
- Confusing the subject of a sentence with the object of a phrase that describes the subject.

Replay

Briefly review the singular and plural forms of some regular and irregular nouns and verbs. Then, alternate writing common and proper nouns and verbs on the board and having students create simple sentences with the words, for example, *Mice* <u>*nibble*</u>, <u>*Lava*</u> *has oozed.* Be creative in your word choices, and encourage your students to do the same.

As students share their sentences with the rest of the class, have them identify the subjects and verbs. Ask the other students if each subject and verb agrees.

Troubleshoot

Share these tips with your class.

✓ Imperatives—*Go! Tell me. Let's talk.*—are complete sentences. The subject *you* is understood—*You go! You tell me. You let us talk.*

✓ Students are sure to encounter sentence fragments in published works of fiction and nonfiction. Writers often use fragments for emphasis or to indicate stream-of-consciousness. You may want to broach the subject yourself and bring in several examples. After students read the examples, discuss why they think the authors chose to use fragments instead of complete sentences. Do students think the authors' choices were successful? Challenge them to revise the writing to include complete sentences and then to compare the revisions to

the original work. Which do they think conveys the author's message better? Students will certainly want to know why published writers can use sentence fragments, while they can't in their own writing. Explain the importance of mastering the fundamentals of sentences before experimenting with the form.

✓ In a sentence like *Each of the dogs comes when I call,* students often confuse *dogs* as the subject instead of *Each*. Remind them to pull out the phrase (*of the dogs*), and then identify the subject and verb in the remaining sentence (*Each comes when I call*).

Model

Distribute the passage "All in a Day's Work," and read it aloud as students follow on the reproducible. Ask students to comment on the content of the story. Then, point out that there are many errors in subject and verb agreement in the story. Find out what students' reactions were to the errors. Did they notice them? Did the errors cause them to slow their reading?

Think aloud to show how and why the correction on the page was made. You might say something like the following: *I see that there is an error in the second sentence. The pronoun "she" is singular, but the verb "know" is plural. I know. You know. She knows. He knows. They know. I would add an "s" to "know" to make it singular and to agree with the subject.*

Teamwork: **Subject-Verb Agreement**

Read the following fictional passage.
Reminder: Sometimes a phrase will separate the subject from the verb.

None of us want a cracker.

None of us *wants* a cracker.

All in a Day's Work

Kyra hopes her mother will forget what day tomorrow is. She know^s it's hopeless because her mother never forgets anything. Miles and Charlotte was taking the train into the city. Jared was going to the firehouse. Lee was visiting the hospital. Kyra sighs. She was going to school, like she did every Thursday.

In the kitchen, a huge calendar almost fills one wall. Kyra can't ignore the green box drawn around tomorrow's date and her mother's precise printing: Take Your Daughter to Work Day. Miles and Charlotte's mom are a lawyer. Jared's mom a firefighter and paramedic. Lee's mom is a nurse. Kyra sighs. Her mom's a kindergarten teacher.

Kyra's grandmother Dede remove the lid from a pot on the stove. "Mmmmm, smell that!" Then she opens the oven door, and the odor of homemade rolls escape.

"Maybe I should go to work with Dad tomorrow," Kyra says. "I had a lot of fun the last two years at the newspaper with him. Mom even say that my writing skills improved after I went to work with Dad."

Kyra's mother rushes through the back door. She's carrying several paper bags and have a big smile on her face. "I'm so excited you're coming to school with me tomorrow! We're going to have so much fun! I've got lots of things planned for us to do."

Both Miles and Jared always said what a good teacher Kyra's mom were. For the first time, Kyra feel curious about what makes her mother such a good teacher. Maybe she'll learn a lot tomorrow in her mom's classroom.

Do you notice any problems in this passage? Does each sentence contain a subject and a verb? Do the subjects and verbs agree with each other? Is the writing as clear as it could be?

Reread the passage. Then mark any errors you spot or any corrections you would make. The first change has been made for you.

Teamwork: **Subject-Verb Agreement**

Read the checklist at the bottom of the page, and go over your revision once more.
Then, copy your revision of "All in a Day's Work" on the lines below.

_____

_____

_____

_____

_____

_____

_____

_____

_____

_____

_____

_____

_____

_____

_____

_____

_____

_____

_____

_____

_____

_____

Checklist ·

❑ Is each sentence complete?
❑ Does it contain a subject and a verb?
❑ Does each subject agree with its verb?
❑ Have you correctly identified the subject of each sentence?

Revision Mini-Lessons • Grade 6 • Scholastic Teaching Resources

Between You and Me: NOUN-PRONOUN AGREEMENT

| **Passage** | "The Third Wright Brother" (nonfiction: biography) | **Curriculum Area** | Social Studies |

Imagine how repetitive our language would be if it didn't contain pronouns. We'd be forced to use the same nouns over and over again, which would affect the variety and flow of our speech and writing.

Your students may encounter the following problems when they integrate pronouns into their writing:

- Choosing the wrong pronoun to replace a noun.
- Neglecting to balance the replacement of nouns and pronouns.
- Failing to make sure the reader knows to whom or what the pronoun refers.

Replay

For a quick review, copy this chart of subjective and objective pronouns on the board. As you go through the chart, ask volunteers to supply sentences for the pronouns. Also review the possessive pronouns.

Subject Pronouns		Object Pronouns	
Singular	**Plural**	**Singular**	**Plural**
1st person:	1st person:	1st person:	1st person:
I	we	me	us
2nd person:	2nd person:	2nd person:	2nd person:
you	you	you	you
3rd person:	3rd person:	3rd person:	3rd person:
he, she, it	they	him, her, it	them

Singular Possessive Pronouns	Plural Possessive Pronouns
1st person: my	1st person: our
2nd person: your	2nd person: your
3rd person: his, her, its	3rd person: their

Then, write the sentences below on the board. Have students copy them on a sheet of paper. They'll be revising each sentence, so ask them to leave several blank lines between each one.

"Perla would love to come to Bill's party," Perla told Bill. At another store, Perla found a baseball hat that Perla thought would be perfect for Bill. The hat looked exactly like the hat Bill had lost when the wind blew the hat off of Bill's head. Bill sent an invitation to Bill's birthday party to Perla because Perla was one of Bill's best friends. Perla went to a nearby store to find a special gift for Bill, but the store was closed. The party was being held at the baseball stadium.

Ask students to revise each sentence so it contains at least one pronoun. Next, instruct students to cut apart the sentences and put them together to form a story. What do they think of their pronoun choices now? Do the choices still make sense, or do the sentences need to be revised again? As students share their work with the class, discuss their revision process.

Troubleshoot

Share these tips with your class.

✓ Objective pronouns—*me, her, him, us, them*—are used after prepositions. A common mistake is using a subjective pronoun after a preposition, for example, *The governor shook hands with Tommy and I.* Rephrasing the sentence so it contains only the pronoun can help students see and hear the error: *The governor shook hands with I.* (See pages 24–26 for more instruction on prepositional phrases.)

✓ Reflexive pronouns—*myself, himself, herself, itself, ourselves, themselves*—always refer to a noun or a pronoun in the sentence: *Kate saw herself reflected in the store window.* not *He gave it to myself.*

Model

Read aloud the passage "The Third Wright Brother" to your students. After discussing its content, ask students how the passage sounded to them. Did it seem to have a smooth flow? Did any of the language seem repetitious or boring? Did they catch any errors in grammar as they listened?

Allow students to read the passage silently. After they finish, walk them through the correction given on the page. You might say something like this: *I see an error in the first sentence. The Wright Brothers' names—Orville and Wilbur—occur twice in the sentence. I would revise the sentence to read this way: "If Orville and Wilbur Wright had two other brothers, then why is their sister Katherine known as the third Wright Brother?" To avoid repeating their names, I replaced "Orville and Wilbur's" with the plural possessive pronoun "their."* Also, write the sentence on the board and show students how you would use proofreader's marks to edit it. Then have students tackle the passage on their own, but make sure they know that they can consult with you about any questions.

9

Between You and Me: **Noun-Pronoun Agreement**

Read the following biographical passage.
Reminder: Objective pronouns—*me, her him, us, them*—are used after prepositions.

The Third Wright Brother

Orville and Wilbur Wright had two other brothers, so why is ^ Orville and Wilbur's *their* sister Katharine known as the third Wright Brother? Orville, Wilbur, and Katharine were the youngest children in the Wright family. Katharine felt there was a special bond between her two brothers and she. Orville and Wilbur were shy, but it was easy for Kate Wright to carry on conversations with other people. Her was also the only Wright child to graduate from college. After graduation, she taught literature to high school students. In fact, she often asked other teachers to help Orville and Wilbur as Orville and Wilbur worked on their experimental airplane outside of Dayton, Ohio.

After their successful flight at Kitty Hawk, North Carolina, the Wright Brothers and its knowledge of airplanes were in demand. Unfortunately, in 1908, Orville's plane crashed when its propeller broke. She quit teaching to nurse her brother and take care of his business dealings. At the time, Wilbur was in Paris, trying to sell airplanes to the French themselves. He asked she and him to join him there. She soon charmed the French. European newspapers began calling Kate the third Wright brother because of Kate's social and business successes. The Legion of Honor, one of France's highest honors, was given to all three of they.

Kate Wright was also involved in the Wright Company, the airplane manufacturing company started by her two brothers. Kate became an officer of the company in 1912. In 1926, Kate married Henry Haskell. Two years later, Kate died of pneumonia.

Do you see any problems in the passage? Have the nouns been replaced with the correct pronouns? Does the passage contain a good mix of nouns and pronouns?

Is the writing as clear as it could be?

Reread the passage. Then, mark any changes you would make.

The first change has been made for you.

Between You and Me: **Noun-Pronoun Agreement**

Read the checklist at the bottom of the page, and go over your revision once more.
Then, copy your revision of "The Third Wright Brother" on the lines below.

_____

_____

_____

_____

_____

_____

_____

_____

_____

_____

_____

_____

_____

_____

_____

_____

_____

_____

_____

Checklist

❏ Have you used the correct pronoun to replace each noun?

❏ Have you used the correct form of each pronoun?

❏ Have you introduced a variety of nouns and pronouns in your revision?

❏ Do the pronouns you substituted for nouns make your writing clear?

❏ Do objective pronouns follow prepositions?

Back to the Future: VERB TENSES

Passage "The African Lungfish" (nonfiction: article)

Curriculum Area Science

A change in verb tense is like time travel. An incorrect shift in tense can send someone or something spinning into the future or the past—when all he, she, or it wanted to do was stay in the present.

Your students may encounter the following problems with verb tenses in their writing:

- Using the incorrect verb tense with time markers.
- Shifting verb tenses within a sentence or a paragraph.
- Failing to include all the parts of a verb in a sentence.

Replay

Review the simple verb tenses with students using examples of regular and irregular verbs, such as *walk* and *go*. Then list some of the common auxiliary verbs on the board or an overhead transparency, including *am, is, are, was, were, been, do, does, did, has, have, had, shall, will, can, could, should, would, might*. Ask students to create verb phrases composed of auxiliary verbs and forms of the main verbs *walk* or *go*. Point out that auxiliary verbs, like main verbs, must agree with the subject. Then challenge students to use their verb phrases in sentences. You also may want to review common time markers such as *yesterday, today, tomorrow, at that time, now, for the next two years, before, already, by this time tomorrow*.

For more practice, challenge students with this writing activity: Divide the class into three groups with the time-sensitive names of *Yesterday, Today,* or *Tomorrow*. Ask students to collaborate on a short paragraph using the verb tense that corresponds to their group's name. Everyone will write on the same topic. You might suggest something as straight-forward as writing about class events, or as exotic as imagining their experiences living on the moon or another planet. Remind groups to pay close attention to the verb tenses in their paragraphs. NOTE: For more information about verb tenses in independent and dependent clauses, see page 24.

Troubleshoot

Share these tips with your class.

✓ Many people use the verb *lay* when they mean the verb *lie*. *Lie* means "to rest." *Lay* means "to put." The verb *lay* always requires a direct object: *Lay the sweater on the bed* not *Lay down on the bed*. To further complicate matters, the past tense of *lie* is *lay*: *Yesterday, he lay down on the bed*, not *Yesterday, he laid down on the bed*. This is a case when incorrect usage probably will sound better to your students since they're exposed to it so often in daily speech.

✓ Adverbs such as *often, also, already, always, usually* may interrupt the auxiliary and main verbs: *Samson has always had a ferocious roar*. Encourage students to place adverbs before the verb phrase in their writing. This will make it easier for them to identify the complete verb.

✓ Make sure students understand that compound verbs must be parallel and share the same tense.

Model

Read aloud the passage "The African Lungfish" as students read it silently. Show them how you would approach the correction that appears in the paragraph, for example: *I skimmed the first paragraph and noticed that almost all the verbs are in the present tense. Then I went back to the beginning of the paragraph. The verb tense is correct in the first sentence. The second sentence is not only a compound sentence, but the first part also contains a compound verb. I know that both these verbs should be the same tense, but "dry up" is in the present tense and "turned" is in the past tense. Both verbs should be in the present tense.*

Before students begin reading and correcting the passage on their own, remind them to look for words that might serve as time markers and for auxiliary verbs that might be separated from main verbs.

Name _____ Date _____

Back to the Future: **Verb Tenses**

Read the following article.

Reminder: Many verb tenses combine helping and main verbs: *He is helping us.*

Polly want a cracker now?

I will want one tomorrow.

The African Lungfish

West and South Africa often experience periods of drought. Water holes dry up and turned into mud holes, but this doesn't bother the lungfish. It digs a hole in the mud, lines the hole with mucus, breathes through its mouth, and waited for rain. Sometimes, the lungfish has to wait for several months before it begins to rain. During that time, the mud hardens and traps the lungfish. All it can do is continue to breathe and wait. Lungfish have been known to stay in their mud "cocoons" for up to four years!

African lungfish will resemble eels. They are long—from 60 to 200 cm—and slender. Two lungs give this fish its name and also help it survive in dry weather. As water heats, it contains less oxygen. The lungfish does have gills to help it breathe underwater. However, in warm water, it is forced to go to the surface to breathe in air.

Millions of years ago, the ancestors of lungfish live in India, Europe, and the United States. We know this because people will discover their fossils in these places. The fossils also reveal that the lungfish not changed over time. In fact, lungfish are sometimes calling living fossils.

What will lungfish look like in the future? Will they ever change to adapt to their surroundings? It's doubtful that lungfish will become less aggressive. Usually, they attack anything that moves. Lungfish are also carnivorous. Zoos placing African lungfish in separate tanks from other aquatic animals, and zookeepers are careful to keep their hands away from the fish.

Do you notice any problems in the passage? Are the correct verb tenses used?

Do the verb tenses match the time words in the sentences? Do verb tenses change in the same sentence?

Are any main verbs missing their helping verbs?

Reread the passage. Then, mark any changes you would make.

The first change has been made for you.

Revision Mini-Lessons • Grade 6 • Scholastic Teaching Resources

Back to the Future: **Verb Tenses**

Read the checklist at the bottom of the page, and go over your revision once more. Then, copy your revision of the passage "The African Lungfish" on the lines below.

_____

_____

_____

_____

_____

_____

_____

_____

_____

_____

_____

_____

_____

_____

_____

_____

_____

_____

_____

_____

_____

_____

_____

Checklist

❏ Have you used the correct verb tense in each sentence?
❏ Does the verb tense shift or change in a sentence?
❏ Are any helping verbs missing in the sentences?
❏ Do the subjects and verbs agree?

Revision Mini-Lessons • Grade 6 • Scholastic Teaching Resources

Really Real: ADJECTIVES AND ADVERBS

Passage "Lucy Lariat" (fiction: tall tale)

Curriculum Area Language Arts

Our language would be considerably poorer without adjectives and adverbs. Adjectives round out nouns. Adverbs add spice to verbs, adjectives, and other adverbs.

Your students may encounter the following problems with adjectives and adverbs in their writing:

- Substituting adjectives for adverbs.
- Substituting adverbs for adjectives.
- Choosing the incorrect forms of comparative and superlative adjectives and adverbs.

Replay

Use the charts below to review adjectives and adverbs as necessary with your class.

	ADJECTIVES	ADVERBS
What They Modify	Nouns	Verbs, Adjectives, Adverbs
Questions They Answer	What kind? *Active* puppies romp. How many? Several puppies snooze. Which ones? *Those* puppies romp.	How? The puppies romped *clumsily*. Where? The puppies romped *outside*. When or How Often? The puppies romped *yesterday*. The puppies romped *frequently*.

POSITIVE ADJECTIVES	COMPARATIVE ADJECTIVES	SUPERLATIVE ADJECTIVES
unhappy	unhappier	unhappiest
content	more content	most content
good	better	best

POSITIVE ADVERBS	COMPARATIVE ADVERBS	SUPERLATIVE ADVERBS
lazily	more lazily	most lazily
well	better	best

Then have each student write down a noun and a verb on different index cards or pieces of paper. Challenge them to stretch their vocabularies and come up with precise and descriptive words. Gather their nouns and verbs. After you read aloud a word, ask students to identify what part of speech it is. Give them about 30 seconds to write as many adjectives or adverbs as they can to go with the word. Discuss students' responses in terms of which questions the adjective answers about the noun or which questions the adverbs answer about the verb.

Troubleshoot

Share these tips with your class.

✓ Students may need to be reminded that *scarcely* and *hardly* are negatives. Point out that in the English language only one negative is used in a sentence. (*That clown can hardly stand still*, not *That clown can't hardly stand still. Scarcely any children attended the circus*, not *Scarcely no children attended the circus.*)

✓ Adjectives follow *to be* verbs when they modify the noun before the verb. (*I am happy.*) Adjectives also follow sense verbs or verbs of appearance when they modify the noun before the verb. (*The teacher seems excited about our grades. The principal looks angry about the noise in the hall.*)

✓ The correct usage of *good* and *well* often confuses students. *Good* is an adjective, while *well* is an adverb. Point out, however, that *good* appears with sense verbs and *to be* verbs. (*That movie star lives well*, not *That movie star lives good. I feel so good today*, not *I feel so well today.*)

Model

Explain to students that they will be reading and revising a tall tale, a story that presents a larger-than-life character with exaggerated qualities. Ask students to listen as you read aloud the passage. Then discuss the story. What did students think of the content? As you read, did they catch any adjectives or adverbs that were used incorrectly? Because this is a tall tale, the misuse of *real* and *sure* and other adjectival and adverbial errors may sound correct to students.

Then distribute the passage to the students. Go over the correction on the page with them. You might model your response like this: *There's an error in the first sentence. The word "sure" is an adjective. An adjective modifies a noun. In this sentence, "could twirl and sling" are being modified, and they're verbs. I know that verbs are modified by adverbs, not adjectives. The adverb "surely" should be used in the first sentence.*

Before students copy their revisions, tell them to think about the adjectives and adverbs in the tall tale. Encourage students to replace them with more dynamic words.

Really Real: **Adjectives and Adverbs**

Read the following tall tale.

Reminder *Real* is an adjective; it modifies a noun. *Really* is an adverb; it modifies an adjective.

Lucy Lariat

                    ly

Lucy Lariat sure^could twirl and sling her lariat. Once, a herd of cattle being driven up from Texas stampeded out of control. A stray bolt of lightning hurtled to the ground near the cattle. The animals turned and twisted and ran wildly across the grassy prairie. A cloud of dust rose ominous from the ground.

    Meanwhile, two hundred miles away, Lucy was sleeping soundly. All of a sudden, she sat up. The air smelled more dirty than a polecat. Lucy hated smelling dust in the air. "Something is wrong," she told her pet bobcat, Jelly. (Although Jelly weighed over four hundred pounds, the sight of a spider or its sticky web would make her shake and quake. Jelly hated spiders.) They covered the two-hundred-mile distance in approximately five minutes and near a hundred steps. "Just as I thought—a cattle stampede," Lucy muttered. "This is not well."

    Lucy's stare was long and widely as she took in the shape of the running herd. Then she shook out her rope, which was extreme pliant, and let it fly. The whirr of it sailing through the dusty air sounded like the whirr of hungry grasshoppers. Lucy's aim was truly. Her lariat settled around the herd, she gently cinched the rope, and the cattle came to a suddenly halt. Jelly gave a low growl of real approval.

    The leader of the cattle drive was so grateful that he wanted to give Lucy Lariat a cow as a gift. The cow was bad startled when Lucy lifted it in her wide palm. "Why, I could not hardly do a thing with this animal," Lucy said. "It wouldn't make a dent in my appetite." She set the cow down, and it tottered away to join the rest of the herd.

Do you notice any problems in the passage? Are nouns modified by adjectives? Are verbs, adjectives, and adverbs modified by adverbs?

Is the writing as clear and exciting as it could be?

Reread the passage. Then, mark any changes you would make.

The first change has been made for you.

16

Really Real: **Adjectives and Adverbs**

Read the checklist at the bottom of the page, and go over your revision once more.
Then, copy your revision of the passage "Lucy Lariat" on the lines below.

_____

_____

_____

_____

_____

_____

_____

_____

_____

_____

_____

_____

_____

_____

_____

_____

_____

_____

_____

Checklist

❑ Have you used adjectives to modify nouns?

❑ Have you used adverbs to modify verbs, adjectives, and adverbs?

❑ Do any of the sentences contain a double negative?

❑ Do adjectives follow *to be* verbs?

❑ Do adjectives follow sense verbs *(smell, taste, feel, sound, look)* and verbs
  of appearance *(look, appear)*?

17

Can You See It Now?: VIVID IMAGES

Passage "Stop!" (nonfiction: expository essay)   **Curriculum Area** Social Studies

vivid **adj. 1.** bright and strong: *vivid colors* **2.** forming or giving a clear picture in the mind: *vivid images*

Creating vivid images in writing engages the reader—and the writer. Figurative language, active verbs, and sensory details bring a subject to life, and help give the writer a unique voice.

Your students may encounter the following problems in trying to incorporate vivid images into their writing:

- Using vague language.
- Repeating the same nouns, verbs, adjectives, and adverbs.
- Cluttering their work with unnecessary adjectives and adverbs.
- Overloading their work with descriptive elements.

Replay

Bring in a variety of writing that contains vivid images. As you read a piece aloud, have students shut their eyes and listen. What images came to mind as they heard the writer's language? Students may disagree about the images, and that's a perfect time to point out that each of us is unique. We all view the world in subtly different ways. It's important for students to realize that each one of them brings this uniqueness to his or her own writing. Then, conduct a brainstorming session in which students revise sentences such as the following to make them more vivid: *She is pretty. He went home. It smelled bad.* As an additional challenge, ask students to bring in items for the class to describe in short, vivid paragraphs.

Troubleshoot

Share these tips with your class.

✓ Creating vivid images begins with choosing strong nouns and verbs. Adding adjectives and adverbs to blah nouns and verbs won't do much to brighten a piece of writing. Visual learners and kinesthetic learners may find it frustrating to create vivid word pictures. Encourage them by suggesting they first create a visual or tactile representation of an image. Then discuss students' creative processes with them. To foster a link between the visual or kinesthetic

and the verbal, point out the descriptive words and phrases they use.

✓ If students are in a language rut, send them to the thesaurus. Keep one handy in your writing center for easy reference. Also remind students that they can access a thesaurus on most word processing programs on the computer.

✓ To give students practice with figurative language, assign a simile or metaphor of the week for them to complete; for example, *as dark as <u>bittersweet chocolate</u>* or *the wind in the trees <u>sang</u>*. Post their work on a Figurative Language bulletin board.

Model

In this passage, students will be replacing existing words with more vibrant and precise ones and adding details to make the writing more vivid. Walk them through the correction on the page, which shows the replacement of an adverb: *After reading and thinking about the first sentence, I see something I could do to make it more vivid and descriptive. First of all, I'd replace the adverb "well" with a more exciting adverb, such as "smoothly."* Also, ask students to contribute other vivid adverbs.

A photo of Garrett A. Morgan's traffic signal appears with the passage "Stop!". Encourage students to use the photo to make the description of the signal more clear and vivid. You may also suggest that they visit the Web site **http://inventors/blgas_mask.htm** to see Morgan's illustration of the signal that he turned in with his patent application.

Can You See It Now?: **Vivid Images**

Read the following expository essay.

Reminder: Adding adjectives to a weak noun won't create vivid images. Neither will adding adverbs to a weak verb. Start with strong nouns and verbs.

You're a pretty parrot.

My sleek feathers shine like emeralds.

Stop!

Things didn't go ~~well~~ ∧ smoothly when the first cars appeared on the road. They joined carriages and wagons pulled by horses and bicycle riders on the busy roads. Pedestrians took their lives into their hands as they tried to cross streets. Accidents happened all the time. Then, in 1923, inventor Garrett A. Morgan got a patent for a traffic signal. His invention helped cut down on the number of road accidents.

An accident between a carriage and an automobile made Morgan invent his traffic signal. After seeing the crash, he decided to make traffic safer. The Morgan Traffic Signal didn't look like our traffic lights today. Instead of lights, Morgan's signal was a tall, rotating pole with three lighted signs: "Stop," "Go," and "Stop in all directions" (so all cars would stop and people could cross the street). Bells warned traffic that the post was about to change direction. The traffic signal used power from overhead electrical lines, so it was inexpensive to run.

Some people see a problem and complain that someone should do something about it. Others see a problem and ignore it. It takes someone very special to decide to do solve a problem. Garrett A. Morgan was a problem solver. He helped make the streets safer for everyone.

Do you notice any problems in the passage? Can you picture what the writer describes? Can you use the photo to make the descriptions more vivid? Are the nouns and verbs as strong as they could be?

Do the adjectives and adverbs make the writing more descriptive?

Reread the passage. Then mark any changes you would make.

The first change has been made for you.

Can You See It Now?: **Vivid Images**

Read the checklist at the bottom of the page, and go over your revision once more. Then, copy your revision of the passage "Stop!" on the lines below.

_____

_____
_____
_____
_____
_____
_____
_____
_____
_____
_____
_____
_____
_____
_____
_____
_____
_____
_____
_____

Checklist

❑ Have you replaced weak nouns and verbs with stronger ones?

❑ Do the adjectives really serve the nouns? Do the adverbs contribute to the verbs, adjectives, or adverbs?

❑ Have you used too many adjectives and adverbs?

❑ Is the passage clear? Is it interesting to read?

❑ Will the descriptions help readers picture Morgan's traffic signal and what traffic was like one hundred years ago?

Precise
Be ∧ C̶h̶o̶o̶s̶y̶: WORD CHOICE

Passage	"How I Deciphered $x - 261 = 189$" (nonfiction: journal entry)	Curriculum Area	Math

Word choice is essential in producing clear and vivid writing. A writer's style is reflected in the words he or she chooses.

Your students may encounter the following problems with word choice in their writing:

- Choosing unnecessarily big words instead of shorter and simpler words.
- Using language that sounds forced.
- Repeating words and phrases.
- Inserting unnecessary words.

Replay

There are two important points to keep in mind when you're teaching students about word choice: 1. Searching for just the right word can be a fun and not a burdensome activity 2. A word should sound natural and enhance the student's writing voice.

Write two sentences that have the same meaning on the board. Make one sentence brief but energetic and the other sentence convoluted. You might use the following examples:

> The toothy canine bared its ugly, yellow fangs and consumed the luscious, barbecue-flavored canine treat.

> The German Shepherd snapped up the luscious treat with its sharp, yellow teeth.

Ask students which sentence they think more clearly describes the dog and its actions. Which sentence immediately gave them a vivid mental picture? Challenge them to write their own sentence that conveys the same meaning as the example sentences. As students share their sentences, point out the similarities and differences in their word choice. Also, acknowledge that there can be a fine line between enlarging our vocabulary and choosing words that state exactly what we want to say. In deciding which words to use, we strive to make our writing clear and compelling.

Troubleshoot

Share these tips with your class.

✓ Errors in speech often creep into students' writing. They record what they hear, for instance, *would of, could of, should of, suppose to,* and *use to.* Spend a few minutes reviewing the proper spelling of these

phrases: *would have, could have, should have, supposed to,* and *used to.*

✓ The words—*very, really,* and *quite*—are the equivalent of soda. They contain "empty calories" because often they don't contribute to the strength of a sentence. Write several sentences containing these words on the board. Go over the sentences with the class, and then erase the "empty calorie" words. Ask students how the deletions affect the sentences and to suggest replacement words.

✓ Repeating words and phrases can emphasize key points in a piece of writing. However, it's easy to reuse the same words in a sentence or a paragraph unintentionally. Introduce the editorial mark "rep" for repetition to students. Encourage them to circle repeated words in their writing and mark them as shown below.

(Empress Si-Lin was responsible for) starting the   ⟨Rep⟩
silk industry in China. Thanks to her, mulberry trees
were cultivated. Silkworms were raised and fed
mulberry leaves. Then the silk was reeled in from the
silkworms. (Empress Si-Lin was responsible for)   ⟨Rep⟩
inventing the loom that wove silk into cloth.

Model

Explain to students that word choice is an important part of every type of writing. Peppering their writing with large words can make a reader focus on individual words instead of paying attention to the entire work. Ask students to follow along as you read aloud "How I Deciphered $x - 261 = 189$." Begin your modeling process by discussing the title: *The title doesn't sound right to me. It sounds like the writer wanted to use a fancy word. He or she might have used a thesaurus to find a word to use. That's a good thing to do as long as the synonym goes with the content of the writing and fits the writer's voice. The synonyms should sound natural, not forced. Since this is the explanation of a math problem, I would replace the word "deciphered" with the word "solved." We solve math problems.* To extend the lesson, consider assigning another math topic for students to write about, for instance, how to find the perimeter of a rectangle.

Precise
Be ∧ ~~Choosy~~: **Word Choice**

Read the following entry from a math journal.

Reminder: Big words and a lot of adjectives don't always make your writing clear or compelling.

Is Polly hungering for a round, flat, baked piece of bread?

Polly wants a cracker.

Solved
How I ∧ ~~Deciphered~~ *x* – 261 = 189

To decipher the problem, I had to determine what *x* stands for. It is a variable that stands for another number. Just by perusing the problem, I was able to determine that *x* is greater than 261. I also was able to determine that *x* is greater than 189. I was able to determine this because it is a subtraction problem. When 261 is deducted from a number, the answer is 189.

To demystify the value of *x*, I added 261 to both sides: $x – 261 + 261 = 189 + 261$. I did that to get the variable all by itself. Then I completed the addition: $x = 450$.

To verify my answer, I replaced *x* in the original problem: $450 – 261 = 189$. My answer is correct.

Do you notice any problems in the passage? Is the writing clear?

Could you replace big words with shorter ones? Are any words or phrases repeated too often?

Reread the passage. Then, mark any changes you would make. The first change has been made for you.

Name _____ Date _____

Precise
Be ∧ ~~Choosy~~: **Word Choice**

Read the checklist at the bottom of the page, and go over your revision once more. Then, copy your revision of "How I Deciphered $x - 261 = 189$" on the lines below.

_____

_____

_____

_____

_____

_____

_____

_____

_____

_____

_____

_____

_____

_____

_____

_____

_____

_____

_____

_____

_____

Checklist
❏ Have you used precise language?
❏ Does the writing sound natural?
❏ Can any big words be replaced by shorter words?
❏ Have you repeated any words or phrases?

Revision Mini-Lessons • Grade 6 • Scholastic Teaching Resources

Join Me: PHRASES, CLAUSES, AND CONJUNCTIONS

Passage	"Judging a Pepper's Heat" (nonfiction: descriptive essay)
Curriculum Area	Science

Phrases and clauses give sentences complexity and depth. However, without supplying punctuation or conjunctions to phrases and clauses, sentences may become unintelligible.

Your students may encounter the following problems using phrases, clauses, and conjunctions in their writing:

- Using the wrong preposition with a word.
- Including a subjective pronoun in a prepositional phrase.
- Omitting commas and/or conjunctions to join independent clauses.
- Creating confusion by using dangling or misplaced modifiers.

Replay

Distinguish the difference between phrases and clauses. A phrase is a group of words that does not contain a subject and a verb. A clause is a group of words that may contain a subject and a verb. Use the chart below to review the types of phrases and clauses.

Phrases	Examples
Prepositional phrase	Captain Gregg flew the rocket *around the moon.*
Infinitive phrase	*To gain speed,* she boosted the fuel jets.
Participial phrase	The heat shield, *burned by the jets,* began to melt.
Gerund phrase	The captain enjoyed *maneuvering the ship* around the moon.

Clauses	Examples
Dependent clause	*Because he wanted to sing,* Brandon closed the window.
Independent clause	Brandon sang quietly, but *his neighbor pounded on the wall.*

Point out the commas that set off the phrases and clauses. Make sure students understand that a coordinating conjunction—*and, or, but*—must join two independent clauses. Challenge students to identify the parts of speech that make up the phrases and clauses. Then, write a series of phrases and clauses on the board, preferably with the same theme or topic, and have students create complete sentences out of them. NOTE: In the second mini-lesson on nouns and pronouns, students learned that an objective pronoun always appears after a preposition (see page 9). Review that information as necessary.

Troubleshoot

Share these tips with your class.

- ✓ When they join independent clauses, students often either fail to add a comma before the coordinating conjunction, fail to add the coordinating conjunction, or both. Remedy this by having students identify the subjects and verbs in the sentence. Then ask them to break the sentence into two separate sentences. Guide students in using a coordinating conjunction, and placing a comma before it, to reconnect the sentences.

- ✓ Also, students may inadvertently modify the wrong words with the phrases and clauses they use. Share an example like the following: *After rescuing the swimmer, there was relief.* Ask students who or what was doing the action: *Who or what rescued the swimmer?* Provide several revisions such as the following: *After rescuing the swimmer, the new lifeguard felt relieved. After the new lifeguard rescued the young child, she felt relieved.*

Model

After students read "Judging a Pepper's Heat" to themselves, discuss the content of the essay. Then, call on a volunteer to read it aloud. Ask the student if he or she had any difficulty in reading the essay because of the placement of phrases and clauses. Then discuss with the class whether some of the sentences sounded awkward or confusing to them.

Think out loud about the correction shown on the page. You might say something like the following: *At first, I thought that the correction didn't need to be made. The peppers could have been stored in baskets of different shapes and sizes. Then I read the next sentence, where the author talks about the peppers' different sizes and shapes. I also thought about a wall display in a grocery store. If you have to display items that have different shapes and sizes, the baskets should be the same shape and size so they can be stacked upon each other because the display fills the whole wall. The more I thought about it, and the more I read, the more sense the correction made.* Discuss whether students agree with the correction and understand your thinking. Errors such as this one can be subtle, but they can also change the reader's visual picture in ways the author is unaware of. Then have students reread and revise the essay on their own.

Join Me: **Phrases, Clauses, and Conjunctions**

Read the following descriptive essay.

Reminder: Conjunctions—*and, or, but*—are used to join two independent clauses, but don't forget to place a comma before the conjunction.

Polly say hello, Polly say good-bye.

Polly says hello, *and* Polly says good-bye.

Judging a Pepper's Heat

A huge display of peppers fills one wall of the local grocery store. Peppers /\ are arranged in straw baskets [of all shapes and sizes]. One day, on a shopping trip, I wondered if a pepper's color, shape, or size had anything to do with how hot it was. With my dad's permission, I chose three different kinds of peppers—an Anaheim, a jalapeño, and a habañero. (If you decide to try this project at home don't rub your face after you've handled a pepper trust me on this one.)

When I got home, I unpacked the peppers. I cut open each one wearing plastic gloves, scraped out the seeds, and diced it into small pieces. (Here's another tip from I: Always wear plastic gloves when you're working with peppers!)

Then, I made careful notes about each one. The Anaheim chili was light green and slender. Having been burned before, I used a toothpick to spear a bit of the Anaheim. It tasted warm on my tongue, almost like the sun. But it wasn't hot. The skin of the jalapeño was a smooth dark green, almost black. Its length was two and one-quarter inches. With heat, the tip of my tongue began to tingle immediately. I ate a piece of avocado to cool my mouth. The habeñero's skin was slightly wrinkled, like the Anaheim's. Needing more air, it looked like a bright orange basketball. In length, it measured slightly less than one inch. Boy, was that habañero hot! My eyes started watering, my mom says that my face turned red.

From my observations, I conclude that the smaller a pepper is, the hotter it's likely to be.

Do you notice any problems in the passage? Are the phrases and clauses punctuated correctly? Is it clear who or what they modify? Does a sentence contain two or more independent clauses separated by conjunctions and commas? Is the writing as clear as it could be?

Reread the passage. Then, mark any changes you would make.

The first change has been made for you.

Revision Mini-Lessons • Grade 6 • Scholastic Teaching Resources

Join Me: **Phrases, Clauses, and Conjunctions**

Read the checklist at the bottom of the page, and go over your revision once more.
Then, copy your revision of "Judging a Pepper's Heat" on the lines below.

_____

_____

_____

_____

_____

_____

_____

_____

_____

_____

_____

_____

_____

_____

_____

_____

_____

_____

_____

_____

Checklist

❏ Do objective pronouns appear in the prepositional phrases?

❏ Have you inserted commas in the phrases and clauses that need them?

❏ Are independent clauses separated by a comma and a coordinating conjunction?

❏ Is it clear which words the phrases and clauses are modifying?

Short-Long-Short: SENTENCE CONSTRUCTION AND VARIETY

Passage "Spindletop" (fiction: historical)　　**Curriculum Area** Social Studies

Using the same sentence patterns over and over again is boring. Varying the length of sentences is more exciting. Hmmm—let me try that again. Using the same sentence patterns can bore your readers. If you vary the length and construction of your sentences, your ideas will flow and engage your readers.

Your students may encounter the following problems when it comes to sentence variety:

- Repeating the same sentence pattern.
- Using short, choppy sentences.
- Running or fusing sentences together.
- Creating overly complex sentences.

Replay

Write the following sentences on the board, and then read them aloud:

> *Out of the water, the dolphin jumped. Into the air, it leaped. Into the water, the dolphin dived again. Out of the water, it jumped again. Into the air, the dolphin leaped again.*

Ask students to critique the writing. Encourage them to identify the repeated sentence pattern (prepositional phrase, subject, verb/prepositional phrase, subject, verb, adverb).

Then, divide the class into small groups and have them work together to revise the sentences for more variety. Remind them that varying the sentence construction, using conjunctions to combine sentences, and adding words will create more interesting prose. Allow time for all the groups to share their sentences. Comment on any diversities in the revisions, and also point out any similarities.

Troubleshoot

Share these tips with your class. NOTE: Also see the previous mini-lesson on phrases, clauses, and conjunctions (page 24) for more troubleshooting tips.

✓ Students may have trouble realizing that they're stuck in a sentence rut. Help them see the repeated pattern in their writing by taking apart a paragraph they've written. Have them copy the sentences of the paragraphs, one by one on a sheet of paper,

with a blank line in between each. Guide students as necessary to identify and label the parts of speech in each sentence. You may want to let them use different colored markers to highlight the parts of speech. Keep a folder filled with different sentence constructions in your writing center or create a bulletin board that spotlights fluid writing—either from well-known writers, your own students, or a combination of the two.

✓ To help students connect related sentences, create a reference sheet that lists some subordinating conjunctions, such as *after, although, because, before, if, since, unless, until,* and *when.* Include several samples showing short, related sentences that have been connected with subordinating conjunctions.

✓ Make sure that students don't abandon short sentences altogether. Sometimes, a writer wants to stop the flow of words and jolt the reader. Remind them that a short sentence can be a good way to grab a reader's attention—as long as short sentences are used sparingly for good effect. Sentence variety is as important as word choice.

Model

After students read the passage "Spindletop" to themselves, read it aloud to them. Briefly discuss the content to make sure everyone understands what's happening in the story before they begin their revision. Then model the correction shown on the page. For example, you might say the following: *First, I reread the entire story. Then I went back and looked at each sentence. Right away, I thought I could combine the first two sentences into one: "Peering over the side of her father's truck, Mercedes saw the tall, spindly-legged oil rig on top of the hill." I had to change some of the words when I combined the sentences because I also reordered the structure of the new sentence.* Because of the length of the story, you may want to continue working with the class on more changes.

Short-Long-Short: **Sentence Construction and Variety**

Read the following passage.

Reminder: Conjunctions such as *and* and *because* can connect sentences.

Spindletop

[Peering over the side of her father's truck, Mercedes saw the tall, spindly-legged oil rig on top of the hill.] ∧ ~~Mercedes peered over the side of her father's truck. The tall, spindly-legged oil rig stood on top of the hill.~~ That hill was the only one in the area. Her father said the hill was really a salt dome. Salt pushing its way to the surface, making the earth bulge.

Mercedes had sneaked into the back of the truck before her father left for the oil field. She wanted to see what her father did at work. Mercedes watched as the men lowered the drilling bit into the hole. She knew mud was packed all around the hole. That helped flush out the pieces of rock created by the drilling. It also helped keep the sand from collapsing around the hole. So far, they had drilled down over one thousand feet. They had drilled mostly through hundreds of feet of sand, clay, and silt. So far, no oil.

Suddenly, the men jumped back. Mercedes could see a blackish-brown substance flowing out of the drilling hole. "Oil!" she breathed. "Mud!" the men shouted. Then, pieces of the drilling pipe shot out of the hole. The men began to run. Mercedes covered her eyes. Nothing else happened. She uncovered her eyes. Her father and the other men were going back to work, cleaning up the mess.

Mercedes felt the truck shake. She heard a huge boom. It sounded like the cannon they shot off in Houston before the Fourth of July parade. More mud flew out of the hole. Then a liquid, blackish-green, gushed out. As Mercedes watched, it rose twice as high as the oil rig. Almost 200 feet in the air. The men threw their hats into the air and cheered. "Oil!" they shouted.

The first well at Spindletop produced an average of 100,000 barrels of oil per day. As Mercedes later told her children and grandchildren and great-grandchildren, that was more oil per day than all of the other oil wells in the United States combined. "And I was there," she always reminded them. She displayed the oil-stained blouse, skirt, and shoes she'd been wearing that day.

Do you notice any problems in the passage? Do too many sentences have the same pattern? Are some of the sentences related so they can be combined?

Reread the passage. Then mark any changes or corrections you would make.

The first change has been made for you.

28

Short-Long-Short: **Sentence Construction and Variety**

Read the checklist at the bottom of the page, and go over your revision once more.
Then, copy your revision of "Spindletop" on the lines below.

_____

_____

_____

_____

_____

_____

_____

_____

_____

_____

_____

_____

_____

_____

_____

_____

_____

_____

_____

Checklist ·

❑ Have you used a variety of sentence lengths and constructions?

❑ Are any sentences too short and choppy?

❑ Are any sentences too long and confusing?

❑ If you've combined sentences, have you used a conjunction
   and the proper punctuation?

Revision Mini-Lessons • Grade 6 • Scholastic Teaching Resources

Give Me Your Support: MAIN IDEA AND DETAILS

Passage	"How Much Fencing Does Noelia Need?" (fiction: word problem)	Curriculum Area	Math

A paragraph or an essay without a main idea is like a ship without a rudder. It's likely to go around and around in circles and never get anywhere.

Your students may face the following problems with main ideas and details in their writing:

- Omitting a main idea.
- Failing to state a main idea clearly.
- Including unnecessary or unrelated details.
- Failing to supply enough details to support the main idea.

Replay

Review the definitions of main idea and details. The main idea is exactly what it sounds like: the main, or big, idea of a paragraph or essay. Details support the main idea. Remind students that a main idea appears at the beginning or near the beginning of a paragraph or essay. Present the following main idea and details, and challenge students to write quick paragraphs based on them. Encourage them to add more relevant details.

> **Main Idea:** Sixth graders should be able to vote.
> **Detail:** The president and other elected officials make important decisions about education.
> **Detail:** Students might take more interest in learning about the government.
> **Detail:** Young people are concerned about important issues, too.
> **Detail:** There are more news channels on television today, so kids are smarter.

Write your own paragraph, and display it on an overhead or write it on the board. Think out loud as you focus on identifying the main idea and supporting details. Invite students' thoughts and ideas as you revise your work.

Troubleshoot

Share these tips with your class.

✓ The key to avoiding major revisions to paragraphs and essays is organization. The more students organize their thoughts before writing, the clearer and more coherent their work will be. Use outlines and other graphic organizers to help students collect their thoughts before they begin writing. As a prelude, consider having students free write their thoughts and questions about a topic.

✓ It can be easy for students to spin away from the main idea when they write. They may treat a supporting detail as a main idea and include details to support it instead of the true main idea. *When birds migrate, they use many methods to find their way. Like pilots, they use landmarks, such as rivers and mountains, to fix their position.* <u>*Pilots also use radar and other instruments in their planes to navigate.*</u> *The sun, stars, and the earth's magnetic field all help birds find their way home.* The supporting details must show a strong connection to the main idea. Have students pull out the main ideas and details in their work and plug them into an outline or web to ascertain if all the details support the main idea.

Model

Read aloud the passage "How Much Fencing Does Noelia Need?" and then discuss it with students. Emphasize that it is a word problem. After students read the passage to themselves, ask them to underline the main idea of the passage. In this case, it's the first sentence: *To keep the deer and other animals from eating the plants in her garden, Noelia decided to erect a fence around it.* Read aloud the second sentence, and ask students if it supports the main idea. Some students may feel that it's unnecessary, but point out that it contains a key element in deciding how much fencing is needed; it reveals that the shape of the garden is a circle.

Then, think aloud to show why the third sentence does not support the main idea. Here's a sample: *Although the third sentence has some interesting information about marigolds in it, the sentence doesn't have anything to do with finding out how much fencing Noelia needs for her garden. Deleting it will keep the reader focused on the main idea.* Have students finish editing and revising the paragraph.

Give Me Your Support: **Main Idea and Details**

Read the following math problem.

Reminder: Details must support the main idea.

Spraying your wings with water will keep your feathers beautiful. It's best to spray them in the morning. That's good, because I might forget to do it at night.

Spraying my wings with water will keep my wings healthy and beautiful. It's best to spray them in the morning. Otherwise, the feathers may not dry before I go to sleep.

How Much Fencing Does Noelia Need?

To keep the deer and other animals from eating the plants in her garden, Noelia decided to erect a fence around it. She had used a tractor to clear a large circle on her land so she could plant the marigolds and tomatoes. ~~Marigolds were natural repellents, and they helped keep birds and insects away from the tomatoes.~~ To find out how much fencing to buy, Noelia knew she would have to find the circumference of the circle. She hadn't thought of circles or circumferences in years.

After consulting her old math textbook, Noelia wrote the following formula: $C = 3.14 \times d$. C stood for circumference, 3.14 was the value of *pi*, and *d* stood for diameter. Using a tape measure, she determined that the diameter of the circle was 48 feet. She rewrote the formula, using the information she knew: $C = 3.14 \times 48$. After solving the problem, Noelia knew that she needed 150.72 feet of fencing. She wanted to buy wire fencing. Noelia decided to buy 160 feet of fencing to be sure she'd have enough.

Do you notice any problems in the passage? Is the main idea well stated and easy to identify?

Is the main idea supported by important details?

Reread the passage. Then, mark any changes you would make.

The first change has been made for you.

31

Give Me Your Support: **Main Idea and Details**

Read the checklist at the bottom of the page, and go over your revision once more. Then, copy your revision of "How Much Fencing Does Noelia Need?" on the lines below.

_____

_____

_____

_____

_____

_____

_____

_____

_____

_____

_____

_____

_____

_____

_____

_____

_____

_____

_____

_____

_____

_____

_____

_____

_____

Checklist ·

❑ Is the main idea clear and easy to identify?

❑ Do all the details support the main idea?

❑ Are any details unnecessary?

Is That Clear?: **ORGANIZATION**

No matter what genre students choose, their writing must be clear, concise, and cohesive.

Your students may encounter the following problems with organization in their writing:

- Arranging steps or events out of sequence.
- Failing to use transitional words and phrases or using too many transitions.
- Staying on the topic or theme. (Also see the mini-lesson on Main Idea and Details, page 30.)

Replay

On the day before the mini-lesson, ask students to write down two copies of the lyrics to a favorite song for homework. In one copy, they should leave space between each line of the lyrics. On the day of class, direct them to cut apart one copy of the lyrics line by line. Provide envelopes and have them put the cut-apart lyrics inside. Tell partners to exchange envelopes and try to put the lyrics back together in the proper order. Talk about the strategies students used to piece together the songs.

Also review transitional words and phrases. Create a reference sheet for students that includes some of the more common transitions; include those that indicate similarity, contrast, sequence and order, time, place and position, cause and effect, emphasis, additional support, and conclusion and summary. Work with students in creating a class paragraph that includes transitions. Begin by listing usual events of the school day in random order. Have students arrange the events in the proper sequence and use them, with transition words, to produce a brief paragraph about a typical school day.

Troubleshoot

Share these tips with your class.

✓ To help students plan their writing, have copies of graphic organizers available. Use main idea and details organizers and outlines for their nonfiction writing. Provide sequence or story problem-and-solution graphic organizers for their fiction writing. When students have trouble with clarity and cohesion in a piece of writing, encourage them to complete the appropriate graphic organizer for their work.

✓ Let's face it, students resist reading over their own work. Impress upon them the importance of this step. Not going over their work is like walking out the door without looking in the mirror. They wouldn't walk out the door wearing a pajama top over blue jeans. You might also suggest that students designate a trusted reader, someone in their family or a friend. This reader can alert students to any organization problems.

Model

Read aloud "X-89 Reporting" while students follow along. Discuss the content of the story, emphasizing that even though it is a fantasy, the events still have to flow in a logical order. Guide students in summarizing the story, and write their summary on the board. Give students the opportunity to read the story silently. Then, model the first correction as follows: *As I read, I noticed several references to specific times. That makes sense since this is a report about what happened to X-89 and its crew during the day. It also follows that the events should be presented in order to avoid confusion. The captain reports in at 24:39. He or she then explains what happened first thing in the morning at 6:49. Then the captain jumps to 19:04, the end of the day. However, a lot happened to X-89 during that time. I would move the underlined sentences to the very end of the story. I also see that the second paragraph begins with a reference to the time 14:19. Jumping back and forth in time like that is too confusing. I would use the times to help me put the events in order.* Remind students to insert transitional words and phrases to help organize the events in the story.

Is That Clear?: **Organization**

Read the following fantasy.

Reminder: Be sure your writing clear, make sure to put things in the proper order.

Say "Pretty please." Oh, wait, before that, say "Polly says." Then whistle first.

Whatever you say: Pretty please, Polly says then whistle first.

X-89 Reporting

This is Captain J. B. Ferguson of roving space pod X-89 reporting in. The time is 24:39, one minute to midnight Martian time. My crew and I had quite a time here on the surface of the red planet today.

Promptly at 6:49, First Officer Klein disabled X-89's night shield. She then enabled the ultraviolet light sensor. [At 19:04, after a long day, First Officer Klein re-engaged the night shield. The only light in X-89 came from the purple glow of the instrument panels.]

By 14:19, the sun was barely visible through the red haze. A huge cloud of Martian dust rose between the sun and us. Navigation Officer Chen couldn't avoid running X-89 into a herd of flying tigers. Their red-and-black stripes blended into the atmosphere. I shouted out a warning. The flow of tigers bowled over X-89. We shuddered to a stop when we hit the bottom of the canyon. Our stomachs pitched as the tigers pushed X-89 over the lip of the canyon.

Soon, we were stuck. Signals from our communication cells bounced off the canyon walls and evaporated. Our escape hatch rested against the floor of the canyon. Next, we felt a sudden jolt. Next, the pod began to rise, although this was not due to any of the crews' efforts. When X-89 rolled up and out of the canyon, we saw a chain of flying tigers straining to lift us out. The time was 18:59.

Do you notice any problems in this passage? Is the writing clear and logical? Are the events in order?

Does the passage need more transitional words or phrases?

Reread the passage. Then, mark any errors you spot or corrections you would make. The first change has been made for you.

Revision Mini-Lessons • Grade 6 • Scholastic Teaching Resources

Name _____   Date _____

Is That Clear?: **Organization**

Read the checklist at the bottom of the page, and go over your revision once more.
Then, copy your revision of "X-89 Reporting" on the lines below.

_____

_____
_____
_____
_____
_____
_____
_____
_____
_____
_____
_____
_____
_____
_____
_____
_____
_____
_____
_____

Checklist

❏ Are the events of the story clear?

❏ Do the events unfold in a logical order?

❏ Have you added transitional words and phrases?

Revision Mini-Lessons • Grade 6 • Scholastic Teaching Resources

Hello?: VOICE

Passage "Pass the Verbs, Please" (realistic fiction)

Curriculum Area Language Arts

Like his or her speaking voice, each student's writing voice is unique. We can recognize someone by hearing his or her voice, and we also can recognize someone by reading his or her written work.

Your students may encounter the following problems with voice in their writing:

- Failing to state exactly what they mean.
- Being too wordy.
- Employing an inappropriate voice for the type of writing.
- Using passive verbs instead of active verbs.

Replay

Write several sentences that contain the problems mentioned above on the board or an overhead transparency. Briefly discuss each sentence to make sure students understand the gist of it. Also, guide them to understand what the problem is with each sentence. Then, ask students to paraphrase the sentences for homework. (You might want to model how you would paraphrase a sentence.) Remind students if necessary that paraphrasing is restating a sentence in one's own words.

Reading a work aloud can be an important element in strengthening one's writing voice. As students paraphrase the sentences, they should also read aloud what they have written. Does the language they use sound natural to their ears? Do they trip over any words or phrases? Set aside time the next day for students to share their paraphrases. Point out the differences in their sentences—and be alert for subtle differences in language and phrasing that differentiate students' voices. Here are some sample sentences you might use.

1. *If they came across a wild animal such as a cougar, most people would probably think what had happened.* (failing to state exactly what they mean)

2. *In the vast and extreme wildness of the wilderness, scientists who have spent many years learning about animals spend countless hours tracking the movements of wild animals, including those sleek, carnivorous felines commonly known as cougars.* (wordiness)

3. *Cougars are so boring.* (inappropriate voice)

4. *The cougar had to be tranquilized by the wildlife veterinarian before it could be fitted with a transmitter by the biologist.* (passive verbs)

Troubleshoot

Share these tips with your class.

✓ Clichés can creep into anyone's writing because they are words and phrases we don't have to give any thought to using. Young students can be especially prone to using clichés because they think the phrases give their writing more weight. Give students an example of a cliché such as "as dark as the night." Challenge them to refresh and update the simile by using it in a sentence.

✓ To avoid confusing students as they explore their writing voices, use the term "passive verb" rather than "passive voice." Set up a Passive Verb versus Active Verb bulletin board giving example sentences for each construction; for example, *The baseball was slugged into the outfield by the batter. The batter slugged the baseball into the outfield.* Illustrate the sentences with a drawing of the action. Change the passive sentences daily and challenge pairs of students to collaborate on revised, active sentences and illustrate them.

Model

Read aloud "Pass the Verbs, Please." In this passage, the first section that needs to be changed is underlined, but a change does not appear on the page. The change involves dialogue, and it's important for students to create their own ideas about the characters and what they would say. To help students in revising the dialogue in the story, encourage them to imagine what Mr. Boxer, Aimee, and Carlton look like and how they sound.

Then, model the change on the page for students: *Dialogue can really bring a character to life. I know that the way I give homework assignments sounds different from the way another teacher would. Some people are formal. They might use a phrase like "young ladies and young gentlemen," but Mr. Boxer's dialogue doesn't sound natural to me. It sounds stilted. Also, "be cool" doesn't really fit with the rest of the language in Mr. Boxer's dialogue. What is the teacher really saying to his students? The bell has rung, and some of them are probably bolting from their seats, but he wants to give them a homework assignment. He's telling them that no one is leaving until he says they can.*

NOTE: Although purpose is discussed in the next mini-lesson, students should be able to figure out that the technical information about dialogue in the third paragraph doesn't fit with the voice of the story.

Hello?: Voice

Read the following story.

Reminder: Remember—your writing voice is just as distinctive as your speaking voice.

Pass the Verbs, Please

Mr. Boxer's voice droned on and on. The more her teacher talked, the heavier Aimee's eyelids felt. When the bell rang, he talked right through the noise. <u>"Now, be cool, young ladies and young gentlemen. You are not abandoning this classroom until I bestow my permission upon you."</u>

Aimee's eyes flew open as homework was given by Mr. Boxer. A look was thrown by her to her best friend, Carlton. How would she be able to do the assignment? How would anyone? "How are we supposed to write a short story full of dialogue if we can't use the word *said*? It's impossible," Aimee groaned.

Dialogue means the words spoken by characters in a story or a play. In a story, dialogue is set off by quotation marks.

"Stop grumbling," Carlton scolded. He lowered the top lid of his right eye to show Aimee that he was teasing her. "At least Mr. Boxer is permitting us to include words that indicate action in our stories."

Do you notice any problems with the passage? Does the writer use too many words? Does he or she include too many passive verbs? Does the voice change within the story?

Is the writing as clear as it could be?

Reread the passage. Then, mark any changes or corrections you would make. The first change has been made for you.

Revision Mini-Lessons • Grade 6 • Scholastic Teaching Resources

Hello?: **Voice**

Read the checklist at the bottom of the page, and go over your revision once more. Then, copy your revision of "Pass the Verbs, Please" on the lines below.

_____

_____

_____

_____

_____

_____

_____

_____

_____

_____

_____

_____

_____

_____

_____

_____

_____

_____

_____

_____

_____

Checklist

❑ Is the writing clear?
❑ Do some sentences contain too many words?
❑ Have you used active verbs rather than passive verbs?
❑ Does the voice change within the short story?

Earning Applause: PURPOSE AND AUDIENCE

Passage   "Under the Bridge"
(nonfiction: expository essay)

Curriculum Area   Social Studies

If students went to a basketball tournament and heard a debate over the length of the school year instead, they probably wouldn't stick around. They wouldn't want to listen to the arguments because they'd been anticipating a different experience. This is true with writing, too.

Your students may encounter the following problems with purpose and audience in their writing:

- Wandering from the original purpose of their writing.
- Using an inappropriate tone to convey their purpose.
- Gauging the knowledge of their audience incorrectly.

Replay

Display a variety of print sources for students to examine—for instance, fiction and nonfiction books (picture books, chapter books, young adult and adult novels), different sections of a newspaper, and articles from different special-interest magazines. Ask students to think about who the audience for each source might be and what the author's purpose was in writing it. As they share their thoughts, encourage students to reveal the clues they used to determine purpose and audience.

Briefly review the different purposes a writer may have—to inform, to entertain, and to persuade. Remind students that a writer can have more than one purpose but that the purposes have to mesh comfortably within the writing. Including a joke in an expository essay on corn production may or may not work. If the joke was used to make a point about the topic, the audience would accept it. However, if the joke was included for entertainment value only, the audience probably would become confused and even begin to distrust the writer.

Troubleshoot

Share these tips with your class.

✓ Students tend to lose their writing voices in expository writing. They may feel that reports and informative essays require an excessive formality. Point out that their writing voice should remain distinctive and natural. Using big words simply to impress readers will usually backfire.

✓ The underpinning of all good writing is the author's passion about his or her subject. Whenever possible, try to match writing assignments to students' personal interests. If a subject or topic seems dull and boring to students, work with them to find a personal connection to the material to fuel their enthusiasm.

✓ Every writer can benefit from having a trusted reader. Ideally, this reader becomes familiar with the writer's voice and can detect any language that sounds forced. A trusted reader can also tell whether the intended purpose has been achieved. Have the writer's ideas made the transition from his or her head to the page?

Model

Read aloud "Under the Bridge," or call on volunteers to do so. Discuss the essay, asking students what the author's purpose was in writing it. What kind of audience do they think the writer pictured as he or she was writing? Have them cite examples from the essay to support their answers. Then, model how you would approach the correction shown on the page: *The third sentence of the essay—I personally love bats—has been deleted. I can think of a couple of reasons why this sentence doesn't belong in the essay. First, it's an opinion. This is an expository essay. Its purpose is to inform readers about bats. This sentence is the only opinion in the entire essay. Second, the sentence uses the first person. All the other sentences in the passage are written in the third person. This is a case of the writer's voice intruding. This sentence doesn't go with all the facts that the writer presents. In this piece of writing, it's not important that the writer tells how he or she personally feels about bats. The writer's interest in bats is clear from the text.*

Earning Applause: **Purpose and Audience**

Read the following expository essay.

Reminder: A writer's purpose for writing should always be clear to his or her readers.

I want to teach you how to sing "The Star-Spangled Banner," but I don't really know why.

Then why should I be interested in learning it?

Under the Bridge

Austin is the capital of Texas. It is home to the governor and other politicians, to students and teachers at the University of Texas, to about 700,000 people—and 1,500,000 Mexican free-tail bats. ~~I personally love bats.~~ The Austin bats comprise the largest colony of bats in North America. In fact, watching the bats fly out of their home under the Congress Avenue bridge has become one of Austin's top tourist attractions.

Before the Congress Avenue Bridge was rebuilt in 1980, only a few bats called Austin their home. After the bridge was finished, the bats began moving in by the thousands. It turned out that the underside of the reconstructed bridge was the perfect roost for them. At first, the citizens of Austin weren't happy about the new arrivals to their city. Many people wanted to get rid of the bats. Luckily, BCI was able to convince Austinites that the bats were harmless as long as people didn't try to touch them. Bat Conservation International (BCI) said that bats actually help make the city a more pleasant place to live by eating about 10,000 to 30,000 pounds of insects each year. I myself hate bugs. Bats use echolocation to help them find the bugs.

In the spring, the bats migrate to Austin from central Mexico. They roost under the Congress Avenue Bridge from March until November, when they return to Mexico. During that period, visitors line the bridge at dusk. You'd never get my brother out there—he hates bats! They're soon rewarded by the beautiful sight of more than a million bats streaming out from under the bridge like a dark brown ribbon.

Do you notice any problems in this passage? Can you identify the author's purpose for writing it? Was it written for readers like you?

Is the writing as clear as it could be?

Reread the passage. Then, mark any errors you spot or corrections you would make. The first change has been made for you.

Revision Mini-Lessons • Grade 6 • Scholastic Teaching Resources

Earning Applause: **Purpose and Audience**

Read the checklist at the bottom of the page, and go over your revision once more. Then, copy your revision of "Under the Bridge" on the lines below.

_____

_____

_____

_____

_____

_____

_____

_____

_____

_____

_____

_____

_____

_____

_____

_____

_____

_____

_____

_____

_____

Checklist

❑ Is the purpose of this essay clear? Does the writer want to inform, entertain, or persuade the reader?

❑ Was he or she successful?

❑ Who is the audience? What type of reader does the writer want to reach?

I Before E: PUNCTUATION AND SPELLING

Passage "Do Dogs and Cats Have to Fight?" (nonfiction: narrative essay)

Curriculum Area Science

A writer may have a strong voice and passionate ideas, but readers may not notice— if misspellings and missing punctuation distract them.

Your students may encounter the following problems with punctuation and spelling in their writing:

- Confusing words that are homophones.
- Forgetting to indent paragraphs.
- Failing to capitalize the first word in a sentence and proper nouns.
- Leaving off end punctuation.
- Omitting commas or inserting too many commas.

Replay

Punctuation: Write on the board a series of unpunctuated phrases, and add more words until you and your students have successfully created and punctuated a sentence. The chart below illustrates an example. Repeat this exercise several times, using interrogatory, imperative, exclamatory, and declarative sentences. Use simple and compound sentences.

Unpunctuated	Punctuate
a tennis ball a bag of peanuts and several pencils	a tennis ball, a bag of peanuts, and several pencils
shelleys backpack contained	Shelley's backpack contained
shelleys backpack contained a tennis ball a bag of peanuts and several pencils	Shelley's backpack contained a tennis ball, a bag of peanuts, and several pencils.

Spelling: Review homophones with students. Explain that many English words sound the same or almost the same, but they have different spellings and meanings. Create a chart containing some common homophones, such as *it's/its, they're/their/there, who's/whose, to/too/two,* and *then/than*. Point out the difference in the first three sets of homophones: One of the homophones contains an apostrophe because it is a contraction. Remind students to ask themselves if they want to use a contraction or a possessive pronoun.

Troubleshoot

Share these tips with your class.

✓ Students often are confused about how to punctuate a series of adjectives, for instance, *the new silver trailer.* Should the phrase contain commas—*the new, silver trailer*—or should it remain unpunctuated? Share this rule with students: If the order of the adjectives can be reversed, then they should use commas to separate them. In the case of the phrase above, *the silver new trailer* doesn't sound right, so *the new silver trailer* wouldn't be punctuated.

✓ Punctuating possessive nouns ending in *s* can pose problems, too. There are conflicting rules about this. Some advocate adding only an apostrophe to a singular possessive noun that ends in *s*. Others say to add an apostrophe and an *s*—unless the word following the singular possessive noun begins with an *s: Mars's atmosphere* but *Mars' summer.* Although students should know that there are different opinions about punctuating possessives, for consistency's sake, choose one method of punctuation for your classroom.

Model

Since the focus of this lesson isn't on language, have students read "Do Dogs and Cats Have to Fight?" silently. Then, before discussing the content of the essay with students, remind them that a writer's voice may be personal and informal in this genre. He or she will probably use the first person, but this doesn't mean that the rules of grammar and spelling should be relaxed. Think aloud to show students how you would have discovered the first error: *I see that the first sentence contains a spelling error. The word "fight" is spelled incorrectly; it should be spelled F-I-G-H-T. This is one of those words in English that isn't spelled like it sounds. It does sound as if it should be spelled F-I-T-E. However, I can think of many other similar words— "light," "might," "night," "sight," "tight"—that have the I-G-H-T spelling. Also, remember that we can learn how to spell words like these by doing a lot of reading and seeing the words in print.*

I Before E: **Punctuation and Spelling**

Read the following narrative essay.

Reminder: *Who's* and *Whose* are homophones. The words sound the same, but they have different spellings and different meanings.

Do Dogs and Cats Have to Fight?

Do cats and dogs always have to ∧ ~~fite~~? I wondered about that when my sister came home and asked if she could have a kitten. Bruno, my Border Collie, growled at the sound of the word *kitten*. He loves chasing our neighbor's calico cat up there pecan tree, and it's trunk is scratched from his nails. However, my sister really wanted the kitten, so my parents said I'd have to train Bruno to get along with the new arrival.

After consulting a few books, I came up with a training plan. All dogs have something called a prey drive Before we turned dogs into pets, they had to chase down smaller animals, prey, for food. dogs today still have the instinct to chase and catch things. For Instance, when I throw Bruno's favorite toy—a small rag doll—he chases it, grabs it in his mouth, and then shakes it. That's bruno's prey drive in action. When dogs chase cats, that's their pray drive kicking in, too.

All the books suggested introducing a dog and a cat to one another gradually. First, I put a leash on Bruno and told him, "Sit and stay!" He sat calmly beside me. His tale did begin to wag when my sister brought the kitten into the room. Like the books advised, she and the kitten stayed across the room. I praised, Bruno for being such a good dog by sitting and staying, I could see how much he wanted to lunge across the room, but he didn't.

My sister and I repeeted the activity every day. Each time, she and the kitten moved a little closer to Bruno and me. I only had to exclaim, "No! Leave it!" one time. In no time at all, my sister and the kitten were standing beside Bruno and me. Then I let Bruno walk around the room, but I held on to his leash. By then, he was comfortable with the kitten. He didn't seem to view her as his prey anymore Now, Bruno lets the kitten curl up under his chin when he's napping!

Do you notice any problems in this passage? Are the sentences punctuated correctly? Are there any misspelled words?

Reread the passage. Then, mark any errors you spot or any corrections you would make.

The first change has been made for you.

Revision Mini-Lessons • Grade 6 • Scholastic Teaching Resources

I Before E: **Punctuation and Spelling**

Read the checklist at the bottom of the page, and go over your revision once more. Then, copy your revision of "Do Dogs and Cats Have to Fight?" on the lines below.

_____

_____

_____

_____

_____

_____

_____

_____

_____

_____

_____

_____

_____

_____

_____

_____

_____

_____

_____

_____

Checklist

☐ Are all the sentences punctuated correctly? Do they begin with a capital letter?

☐ Have you used the wrong form of a homophone?

☐ Are any words misspelled?

Revision Mini-Lessons • Grade 6 • Scholastic Teaching Resources

Answer Key Sample revisions are given.

Subject-Verb Agreement, p. 7

All in a Day's Work

Kyra hopes her mother will forget what day tomorrow is. She knows it's hopeless because her mother never forgets anything. Miles and Charlotte were taking the train into the city. Jared was going to the firehouse. Lee was visiting the hospital. Kyra sighs. She was going to school, like she did every Thursday.

In the kitchen, a huge calendar almost fills one wall. Kyra can't ignore the green box drawn around tomorrow's date and her mother's precise printing: Take Your Daughter to Work Day. Miles and Charlotte's mom is a lawyer. Jared's mom is a firefighter and paramedic. Lee's mom is a nurse. Kyra sighs. Her mom's a kindergarten teacher.

Kyra's grandmother Dede removes the lid from a pot on the stove. "Mmmmm, smell that!" Then she opens the oven door, and the odor of homemade rolls escapes.

"Maybe I should go to work with Dad tomorrow," Kyra says. "I had a lot of fun the last two years at the newspaper with him. Mom even says that my writing skills improved after I went to work with Dad."

Kyra's mother rushes through the back door. She's carrying several paper bags and has a big smile on her face. "I'm so excited you're coming to school with me tomorrow! We're going to have so much fun! I've got lots of things planned for us to do."

Both Miles and Jared always said what a good teacher Kyra's mom was. For the first time, Kyra feels curious about what makes her mother such a good teacher. Maybe she'll learn a lot tomorrow in her mom's classroom.

Noun-Pronoun Agreement, p. 10

The Third Wright Brother

Orville and Wilbur Wright had two other brothers, so why is their sister Katharine known as the third Wright Brother? Orville, Wilbur, and Katharine were the youngest children in the Wright family. Katharine felt there was a special bond between her two brothers and her. Orville and Wilbur were shy, but it was easy for Kate Wright to carry on conversations with other people. She was also the only Wright child to graduate from college. After graduation, she taught literature to high school students. In fact, Kate often asked other teachers to help Orville and Wilbur as they worked on their experimental airplane outside of Dayton, Ohio.

After their successful flight at Kitty Hawk, North Carolina, the Wright Brothers and their knowledge of airplanes were in demand. Unfortunately, in 1908, Orville's plane crashed when its propeller broke. Kate quit teaching to nurse her brother and take care of his business dealings. At the time, Wilbur was in Paris, trying to sell airplanes to the French. He asked Kate and Orville to join him there. Kate soon charmed the French. European newspapers began calling her the third Wright brother because of her social and business successes. The Legion of Honor, one of France's highest honors, was given to all three of them.

Kate Wright was also involved in the Wright Company, the airplane manufacturing company started by her two brothers. She became an officer of the company in 1912. In 1926, Kate married Henry Haskell. Two years later, she died of pneumonia.

Verb Tenses, p. 13

The African Lungfish

West and South Africa often experience periods of drought. Water holes dry up and turn into mud holes, but this doesn't bother the lungfish. It digs a hole in the mud, lines the hole with mucus, breathes through its mouth, and waits for rain. Sometimes, the lungfish has to wait for several months before it begins to rain. During that time, the mud hardens and traps the lungfish. All it can do is continue to breathe and wait. Lungfish have been known to stay in their mud "cocoons" for up to four years!

African lungfish resemble eels. They are long—from 60 to 200 cm—and slender. Two lungs give this animal its name and help it survive in dry weather. As water heats, it contains less oxygen. The lungfish does have gills to help it breathe underwater. However, in warm water, it is forced to go to the surface to breathe in air.

Millions of years ago, the ancestors of lungfish lived in India, Europe, and the United States. We know this because people have discovered their fossils in these places. The fossils also reveal that the lungfish hasn't changed over time. In fact, lungfish are sometimes called living fossils.

What will lungfish look like in the future? Will they ever change to adapt to their surroundings? It's doubtful that lungfish will become less aggressive. Usually, they will attack anything that moves. Lungfish are also carnivorous. Zoos place African lungfish in separate tanks from other aquatic animals, and zookeepers are careful to keep their hands away from the fish.

Adjectives and Adverbs, p. 16

Lucy Lariat

Lucy Lariat surely could twirl and sling her lariat. Once, a herd of cattle being driven up from Texas stampeded out of control. A stray bolt of lightning hurtled to the ground near the cattle. The animals turned and twisted and ran wildly across the grassy prairie. A cloud of dust rose ominously from the ground.

Meanwhile, two hundred miles away, Lucy was sleeping soundly. All of a sudden, she sat up. The air smelled dirtier than a polecat. Lucy hated smelling dust in the air. "Something is wrong," she told her pet bobcat, Jelly. (Although Jelly weighed over four hundred pounds, the sight of a spider or its sticky web would make her shake and quake. Jelly hated spiders.) They covered the two-hundred-mile distance in approximately five minutes and nearly a hundred steps. "Just as I thought—a cattle stampede," Lucy muttered. "This is not good."

Lucy's stare was long and wide as she took in the shape of the running herd. Then she shook out her rope, which was extremely pliant, and let it fly. The whirr of it sailing through the dusty air sounded like the whirr of hungry grasshoppers. Lucy's aim was true. Her lariat settled around the herd, she gently cinched the rope, and the cattle came to a sudden halt. Jelly gave a low growl of real approval.

The leader of the cattle drive was so grateful that he wanted to give Lucy Lariat a cow as a gift. The cow was badly startled when Lucy lifted it in her wide palm. "Why, I could hardly do a thing with this animal," Lucy said. "It wouldn't make a dent in my appetite." She set the cow down, and it tottered away to join the rest of the herd.

Answers (Continued)

Vivid Images, p. 19

Stop!

Things didn't go smoothly when the first cars appeared on the road. They joined carriages, horse-drawn wagons, and bicycle riders on the already crowded roads. Pedestrians took their lives into their hands as they tried to cross streets. Accidents happened all the time. Then, in 1923, inventor Garrett A. Morgan got a patent for a traffic signal. His invention helped cut down on the number of road accidents.

An accident between a carriage and an automobile inspired Morgan to invent his traffic signal. After witnessing the terrible impact of the crash, he vowed to make traffic safer. The Morgan Traffic Signal didn't look like our traffic lights of today. Instead of red, yellow, and green lights, Morgan's signal was a tall, rotating pole with three lighted signs: "Stop," "Go," and "Stop in all directions" (so all cars would stop and pedestrians could cross the street). Clanging bells warned traffic that the post was about to change direction. The traffic signal used power from overhead electrical lines, so it was inexpensive to run.

Some people see a problem and complain that someone should do something about it. Others see a problem and ignore it. It takes someone very special to decide to solve a problem. Garrett A. Morgan was a problem solver. He helped make the streets safer for drivers, passengers, and pedestrians.

Word Choice, p. 22

How I Solved $X - 261 = 189$

To solve this problem, I had to find out what x stands for. It is a variable that stands for another number. Just by looking at the problem, I knew that x was greater than 261. Also, I knew that x is greater than 189 because it was a subtraction problem. When 261 is taken away from a number, the answer is 189.

To find the value of x, I added 261 to both sides: $x - 261 + 261 = 189 + 261$. I did that to get the variable all by itself. Then I completed the addition: $x = 450$.

To check my answer, I replaced x in the original problem: $450 - 261 = 189$. My answer is correct.

Phrases, Clauses, and Conjunctions, p. 25

Judging a Pepper's Heat

A huge display of peppers fills one wall of the local grocery store. Peppers of all shapes and sizes are arranged in straw baskets. One day, on a shopping trip, I wondered if a pepper's color, shape, or size had anything to do with how hot it was. With my dad's permission, I chose three different kinds of peppers—an Anaheim, a jalapeño, and a habañero. (If you decide to try this project at home, don't rub your face after you've handled a pepper. Trust me on this one.)

When I got home, I unpacked the peppers. Wearing plastic gloves, I cut open each pepper, scraped out the seeds, and diced it into small pieces. (Here's another tip from me: Always wear plastic gloves when you're working with peppers!)

Then, I made careful notes about each one. The Anaheim chili was light green and slender. Having been burned before, I used a toothpick to spear a bit of the Anaheim. It tasted warm on my tongue, almost like the sun, but it wasn't hot. The skin of the jalapeño was a smooth dark green, almost black. Its length was two and one-quarter inches. The tip of my tongue began to tingle with heat immediately. I ate a piece of avocado to cool my mouth. The habañero's skin was slightly wrinkled, like the Anaheim's. It looked like a bright orange basketball that needed more air. In length, it measured slightly less than one inch. Boy, was that habañero hot! My eyes started watering, and my mom says that my face turned red.

From my observations, I conclude that the smaller a pepper is, the hotter it's likely to be.

Sentence Construction and Variety, p. 28

Spindletop

Peering over the side of her father's truck, Mercedes saw the tall, spindly-legged oil rig on top of the hill. That hill was the only one in the area. Her father said it was really a salt dome. Salt was pushing its way to the surface, making the earth bulge.

Mercedes had sneaked into the back of the truck before her father left for the oil field. She wanted to see what her father did at work. Now she watched as the men lowered the drilling bit into the hole. She knew mud was packed all around the hole. That helped flush out the pieces of rock created by the drilling. It also helped keep the sand from collapsing around the hole. So far, they had drilled down over one thousand feet, mostly through hundreds of feet of sand, clay, and silt. So far, there was no oil.

Suddenly, the men jumped back. Mercedes could see a blackish-brown substance flowing out of the drilling hole. "Oil!" she breathed. "Mud!" the men shouted. Then, pieces of the drilling pipe shot out of the hole. The men began to run. Mercedes covered her eyes, but nothing else happened. She uncovered her eyes. Her father and the other men were going back to work, cleaning up the mess.

Suddenly Mercedes felt the truck shake. She heard a huge boom. It sounded like the cannon they shot off in Houston before the Fourth of July parade. More mud flew out of the hole. Then a liquid, blackish-green, gushed out. As Mercedes watched, it rose almost 200 feet in the air, twice as high as the oil rig. The men threw their hats into the air and cheered. "Oil!" they shouted.

That first well at Spindletop produced an average of 100,000 barrels of oil per day. As Mercedes later told her children and grandchildren and great-grandchildren, that was more oil than all of the other oil wells in the United States combined. "And I was there," she always reminded them as she displayed the oil-stained blouse, skirt, and shoes she'd been wearing that day.

Answers (Continued)

Main Idea and Details, p. 31

How Much Fencing Does Noelia Need?

To keep the deer and other animals from eating the plants in her garden, Noelia decided to erect a fence around it. She had used a tractor to clear a large circle on her land so she could plant marigolds and tomatoes. To find out how much fencing to buy, Noelia knew she would have to find the circumference of the circle.

After consulting her math textbook, Noelia wrote the following formula: $C = 3.14 \times d$. C stood for circumference, 3.14 was the value of pi, and d stood for diameter. The diameter of the circle was 48 feet. She rewrote the formula, using the information she knew: $C = 3.14 \times 48$. After solving the problem, Noelia knew that she needed 150.72 feet of fencing. She decided to buy 160 feet of fencing so she'd have enough.

Organization, p. 34

X-89 Reporting

This is Captain J. B. Ferguson of roving space pod X-89 reporting in. The time is 24:39, one minute to midnight Martian time. My crew and I had quite a time here on the surface of the red planet.

Promptly at 6:49, First Officer Klein disabled X-89's night shield. She then enabled the ultraviolet light sensor. By 14:19, the sun was barely visible through the red haze. A huge cloud of Martian dust rose between the sun and us. I shouted out a warning, but Navigation Officer Chen couldn't avoid running X-89 into a herd of flying tigers. Their red-and-black stripes blended into the atmosphere. The flow of tigers bowled over X-89. Our stomachs pitched as the tigers pushed the pod over the lip of the canyon. We shuddered to a stop when we hit the bottom of the canyon.

Next, we felt a sudden jolt. Our escape hatch rested against the floor of the canyon. We were stuck. Signals from our communication cells bounced off the canyon walls and evaporated. Suddenly, the pod began to rise, although this was not due to any of the crews' efforts. When X-89 rolled up and out of the canyon, we saw a chain of flying tigers straining to lift us out. The time was 18:59.

At 19:04, after a long day, First Officer Klein re-engaged the night shield. The only light in X-89 came from the purple glow of the instrument panels.

Voice, p. 37

Pass the Verbs, Please

Mr. Boxer's voice droned on and on. The more her teacher talked, the heavier Aimee's eyelids felt. When the bell rang, he talked right through the noise. "Now, slow down, young ladies and gentlemen. You're not leaving this room until I say you can."

Aimee's eyes flew open as Mr. Boxer assigned their homework. She threw a look to her best friend, Carlton. How would she be able to do the assignment? How would anyone be able to do it? "How are we supposed to write a short story full of dialogue if we can't use the word *said*? It's impossible," Aimee groaned.

"Stop grumbling," Carlton teased. He winked to show Aimee that he was teasing her. "At least Mr. Boxer's letting us use verbs in our stories."

Purpose and Audience, p. 40

Under the Bridge

Austin is the capital of Texas. It is home to the governor and other politicians, to students and teachers at the University of Texas, to about 700,000 people—and to 1,500,000 Mexican free-tail bats. The Austin bats comprise the largest colony of bats in North America. In fact, watching the bats fly out of their home under the Congress Avenue Bridge has become one of Austin's top tourist attractions.

Before the Congress Avenue Bridge was rebuilt in 1980, only a few bats called Austin home. After the bridge was finished, the bats began moving in by the thousands. It turned out that the underside of the reconstructed bridge was the perfect roost for them. At first, the citizens of Austin weren't happy about the new arrivals to their city. Many people wanted to get rid of the bats. Luckily, Bat Conservation International (BCI) was able to convince Austinites that the bats were harmless as long as people didn't try to touch them. BCI said the bats actually help make the city a more pleasant place to live by eating about 10,000 to 30,000 pounds of insects each year.

In the spring, the bats migrate to Austin from central Mexico. They roost under the Congress Avenue Bridge from March until November, when they return to Mexico. During that period, visitors line the bridge at dusk. They're soon rewarded by the beautiful sight of more than a million bats streaming out from under the bridge like a dark brown ribbon.

Punctuation and Spelling, p. 43

Do Dogs and Cats Have to Fight?

Do cats and dogs always have to fight? I wondered about that when my sister came home and asked if she could have a kitten. Bruno, my Border Collie, growled at the sound of the word *kitten*. He loves chasing our neighbor's calico cat up their pecan tree, and its trunk is scratched from his nails. However, my sister really wanted the kitten, so my parents said I'd have to train Bruno to get along with the new arrival.

After consulting a few books, I came up with a training plan. All dogs have something called a prey drive. Before we turned dogs into pets, they had to chase down smaller animals, prey, for food. Dogs today still have the instinct to chase and catch things. For instance, when I throw Bruno's favorite toy—a small rag doll—he chases it, grabs it in his mouth, and then shakes it. That's Bruno's prey drive in action. When dogs chase cats, that's their prey drive kicking in, too.

All the books suggested introducing a dog and a cat to one another gradually. First, I put a leash on Bruno and told him, "Sit and stay!" He sat calmly beside me. His tail did begin to wag when my sister brought the kitten into the room. Like the books advised, she and the kitten stayed across the room. I praised Bruno for being such a good dog by sitting and staying. I could see how much he wanted to lunge across the room, but he didn't.

My sister and I repeated the activity every day. Each time, she and the kitten moved a little closer to Bruno and me. I only had to exclaim, "No! Leave it!" one time. In no time at all, my sister and the kitten were standing beside Bruno and me. I let Bruno walk around the room, but I held on to his leash. By then, he was comfortable with the kitten. He didn't seem to view her as his prey anymore. Now, Bruno lets the kitten curl up under his chin when he's napping!

Writing Checklist

Subject-Verb Agreement
❑ Is each sentence complete? Does it contain a subject and a verb?
❑ Does each subject agree with its verb?
❑ Have you correctly identified the subject of each sentence?

Noun-Pronoun Agreement
❑ Have you used the correct pronoun to replace each noun?
❑ Have you used the correct form of each pronoun?
❑ Does this revised passage contain a variety of nouns and pronouns?
❑ Do the pronouns you substituted for nouns make your meaning clear?

Verbs
❑ Have you used the correct verb tense in each sentence?
❑ Does the verb tense shift or change in a sentence?
❑ Are any helping verbs missing in the sentences?
❑ Do the subjects and verbs agree?

Adjectives and Adverbs
❑ Do the adjectives modify nouns?
❑ Do the adverbs modify verbs, adjectives, or adverbs?
❑ Do any of the sentences contain a double negative?
❑ Do adjectives follow *to be* verbs *(is, was)*?
❑ Do adjectives follow sense verbs *(smell, taste, feel, sound, look)* and verbs of appearance *(look, appear)*?

Vivid Language
❑ Have you replaced weak nouns and verbs with stronger ones?
❑ Do the adjectives really serve the nouns?
❑ Do the adverbs contribute to the verbs, adjectives, or adverbs? Have you used too many adjectives and adverbs?
❑ Is the passage clear? Is it interesting to read?

Word Choice
❑ Have you used precise language?
❑ Does your writing sound natural?
❑ Can any big words be replaced by shorter words?
❑ Have you repeated any words or phrases?

Phrases, Clauses, and Conjunctions
❑ Do prepositional phrases begin with the correct preposition? Do they end with nouns or objective pronouns?
❑ Is it clear which word each phrase is modifying?
❑ Have you combined subjects, verbs, and sentences whenever you could? Have you used the correct conjunction?
❑ Have you placed a comma before a conjunction that joins two sentences?

Sentence Variety
❑ Have you used a variety of sentences?
❑ Are too many sentences short and choppy?
❑ Are any sentences too long and confusing?
❑ If you've combined sentences, have you used a conjunction and the proper punctuation?

Main Idea and Details
❑ Is the main idea clear and easy to identify?
❑ Do all the details support the main idea?
❑ Are any details unnecessary?

Organization
❑ Are the events or steps clear and in order?
❑ Have you added transitional words and phrases?

Voice
❑ Do some sentences contain too many words?
❑ Does some language sound forced?
❑ Does the voice change within the passage?

Purpose and Audience
❑ Is the purpose of the piece of writing clear? Do you want to inform, entertain, or persuade?
❑ Who is your audience? What type of reader do you want to reach?

Punctuation and Spelling
❑ Is each sentence punctuated correctly? Does it begin with a capital letter? Does it end with the correct punctuation?
❑ Have you used the wrong word or homophone?
❑ Are any words misspelled?